D0475273

THE DANGERS OF DRUGS, ALCOHOL, AND SMOKING

THE DANGERS OF
ILLEGAL
DRUGS

CHRISTINE HONDERS

PowerKiDS
press.
New York

Published in 2020 by The Rosen Publishing Group, Inc.
29 East 21st Street, New York, NY 10010

First Edition

Editor: Jenna Tolli
Book Design: Reann Nye

Photo Credits: Cover Tetra Images/Brand X Pictures/Getty Images; series art patpitchaya/Shutterstock.com; p. 5 Blamb/Shutterstock.com; p. 6 CHAjAMP/Shutterstock.com; p. 7 Ariel Skelley/DigitalVision/Getty Images; p. 9 fstop123/E+/Getty Images; p. 11 Daisy Daisy/Shutterstock.com; pp. 13, 22 Monkey Business Images/Shutterstock.com; p. 15 Tetra Images/Getty Images; p. 16 Greentellect Studio/Shutterstock.com; p. 17 Iakov Filimonov/Shutterstock.com; p. 18 skifbook/Shutterstock.com; p. 19 Rido/Shutterstock.com; p. 21 Zinkevych/iStock/Getty Images Plus/Getty Images.

Library of Congress Cataloging-in-Publication Data

Names: Honders, Christine, author.
Title: The dangers of illegal drugs / Christine Honders.
Description: New York : PowerKids Press, 2020. | Series: The dangers of
  drugs, alcohol, and smoking | Includes index.
Identifiers: LCCN 2019018539| ISBN 9781725309746 (pbk.) | ISBN 9781725309760
  (library bound) | ISBN 9781725309753 (6 pack)
Subjects: LCSH: Drug abuse–Juvenile literature.
Classification: LCC HV5809.5 .H64 2020 | DDC 613.8–dc23
LC record available at https://lccn.loc.gov/2019018539

Manufactured in the United States of America

Some of the images in this book illustrate individuals who are models. The depictions do not imply actual situations or events.

CPSIA Compliance Information: Batch #CWPK20. For Further Information contact Rosen Publishing, New York, New York at 1-800-237-9932.

CONTENTS

WHAT ARE DRUGS?

Drugs are **chemicals** that change the way your brain and body work. They can also change the way you think and feel. Some drugs can save lives and cure illnesses. When someone has a problem using drugs, that usually means they're taking illegal drugs.

Illegal drugs are **addictive**, meaning that once you start using them, it's very hard to stop. Being addicted to illegal drugs can cause you to make bad decisions and put your health at risk. Knowing the dangers of illegal drugs can help you make the right choice to stay away from them and live a healthy lifestyle.

DANGER ZONE

Doctors give people **medication** for pain. But some people take the medication when they don't need it, or take too much at once. This is very dangerous, or unsafe.

Different parts of the brain are affected by drugs. The dark pink area is the part that makes us feel good.

LEGAL DRUGS VS. ILLEGAL DRUGS

Medicines are legal drugs that can be bought in stores. Doctors are allowed to **prescribe** them and people are allowed to take them. Illegal drugs are against the law for everyone. They include crystal meth, ecstasy, cocaine, heroin, and LSD. It's also against the law to **abuse** prescribed drugs.

DANGER ZONE

Some studies show that marijuana helps people with pain, stomach problems, and even **cancer**. More studies need to be done to know whether it is effective and safe to use.

Cigarettes and alcohol are legal drugs for adults, but against the law for kids. Adults who smoke or drink too much can suffer from many health problems. In some states, marijuana is legal if it is taken for medical reasons. Other states have made it legal for personal use.

ILLEGAL DRUGS ARE HARMFUL

Illegal drugs are harmful for everyone. They can **damage** the heart, brain, and lungs. Illegal drugs are especially dangerous for children and teenagers, whose bodies are still growing.

Cocaine can cause heart attacks, even in teenagers. Illegal drugs can also cause strokes, which happen when blood can't get to the brain. Strokes can take away your ability to walk, talk, and think. Some people die the first time they take illegal drugs.

People who abuse drugs have a hard time thinking clearly and making good decisions. They might do unsafe things when they use drugs. They also have trouble with school, sports, and other activities.

People that use drugs might start to do things they would not normally do. They might get into fights, want to be alone a lot, or start to be friends with other people that use drugs.

WHY PEOPLE TAKE ILLEGAL DRUGS

People might take drugs because they aren't happy or they want to change something in their lives. People who are sad may take drugs to make the bad feelings go away. They might feel better for a little while when they use drugs, but when the drug's effects wear off, the problems are still there.

Kids and teenagers might take drugs to fit in. Some kids take drugs to go against their parents or break the rules. Others take drugs because they're curious or bored. If you are feeling this way, talk to an adult you trust. You can make good decisions about not using illegal drugs.

Teens may have friends who make them feel bad for not trying illegal drugs. Good friends stick together and support each other's decisions.

>

11

ADDICTION

When a person abuses an illegal drug, their body starts to depend on it. The person becomes so used to taking the drug every day that they can't do anything without it. This is called addiction.

Once someone is addicted to a drug, it's very hard for them to stop. If they do stop, they can get very sick. When people are addicted to drugs and try to quit, they often suffer through days or weeks of sweating, throwing up, and uncontrollable shaking. Many times, they feel so sick that they go back to doing the drug to make the suffering go away.

DANGER ZONE

Some signs that someone you know might be using drugs include: loss of interest in activities and friends, red or puffy eyes, major mood changes, and increased sleepiness.

Some drugs are very addictive.
Even after using a drug just once
or twice, someone might find it
hard to stop.

TYPES OF DRUGS

Drugs can be grouped into different **categories**, depending on how they affect the people that use them.

- *Stimulants* speed up body activity. They can give those using them more energy.

- *Hallucinogens* cause people to see and hear things that aren't there. These effects can come back for a long time after using the drugs.

- *Depressants* slow down body activity. They can make people feel relaxed and less worried.

- *Opioids* are strong painkillers. Doctors prescribe some opioids for pain for a short time. When these drugs are misused, it can lead to illegal opioid use.

DANGER ZONE

Some drugs fit into multiple categories. For example, effects from marijuana fit into the depressant, hallucinogen, and stimulant categories.

Legal drugs can be grouped under these categories too. When people have trouble sleeping, doctors might prescribe a depressant medication to help.

STIMULANTS

Crystal meth is a stimulant that gives those using it a quick and lasting **high**. It's a clear rock that's usually smoked. Those using it feel an increase in energy and confidence. Crystal meth also causes mood swings and changes in sleeping patterns. Longtime use can cause strange behavior, mental health problems, confusion, or strokes.

COCA PLANT

16

Cocaine is a stimulant made from coca plants. It's a white powder that is **inhaled** through the nose or taken using a needle. Cocaine causes high happiness and energy, but the effects do not last long. Cocaine raises the heartbeat so fast that it can lead to a heart attack or stroke.

Ecstasy is a stimulant and hallucinogen that comes in different colored pills or tablets. It gives those using it a high, and makes good or bad feelings stronger. It can also cause feelings of sickness or dizziness. Ecstasy is especially dangerous because drug dealers add other deadly drugs and chemicals to the pills to make them stronger.

DANGER ZONE

Some hallucinogens are found in plants and mushrooms. Peyote, shown here, is a type of cactus that creates a hallucinogen. Other hallucinogens are made in laboratories.

LSD is a powerful hallucinogen. It's a clear liquid taken by mouth. Those who use it can have strange emotions and feelings. Some might see brighter colors or feel that time is moving more slowly. Others report "bad trips," which include strong feelings of fear and panic.

DEPRESSANTS AND OPIOIDS

Marijuana's effects can look like those from stimulants, hallucinogens, or depressants. Marijuana comes from a plant that is dried and smoked. Marijuana is legal in some places and can be used to help certain medical problems. People who abuse this drug can suffer from memory loss, lung damage, and other issues.

Heroin is an opioid made from the seeds of opium poppy plants. It can be inhaled, smoked or taken by a needle. A person using it can experience a rush of good feelings and a relief from bodily pain. However, it also slows down heartbeat and breathing, which can lead to a deadly **overdose**.

DANGER ZONE

Drugs like heroin and cocaine are very dangerous. Trying these drugs just once can lead to an addiction.

When someone is addicted to drugs, it affects their whole family. They may spend less time with family members and forget important responsibilities.

GETTING HELP

There are different ways to help people if they have a problem using illegal drugs. Doctors and therapists work with people to help them quit. People who are addicted to drugs can join support groups, where members help each other stay away from drugs. Some medications can keep people living with a drug addiction from getting sick while they're starting to quit.

If you think someone is using illegal drugs, tell an adult you trust. They can help find what kind of treatment, or medical care, the person might need. The best way to keep yourself safe from the dangers of illegal drugs is to never try them.

GLOSSARY

abuse: To treat or use something in a wrong or unfair way; also, the act of doing so.

addictive: A strong to harmful need to regularly do something.

cancer: A serious disease caused by abnormal cells that can spread to parts of the body.

categories: A group of similar things.

chemical: Matter that can be mixed with other matter to cause changes.

damage: Loss or harm done to a person or object.

high: Intoxicated or affected by alcohol or drug use.

inhale: To breathe in.

medication: A substance used to treat a medical problem or to relieve pain.

overdose: Too much of a substance like a medicine or illegal drug that is dangerous.

prescribe: To officially tell someone to use a medicine or treatment.

INDEX

WEBSITES

Due to the changing nature of Internet links, PowerKids Press has developed an online list of websites related to the subject of this book. This site is updated regularly. Please use this link to access the